A Kid's Guide
to the
Classification
of
Living Things™

Animals
With
Backbones

Elaine Pascoe

Photographs by Dwight Kuhn

The Rosen Publishing Group's
PowerKids Press™
New York

Published in 2003 by The Rosen Publishing Group, Inc.
29 East 21st Street, New York, NY 10010

First Edition

Editor: Natashya Wilson
Book Design: Emily Muschinske
Layout: Eric DePalo

Photo Credits: All photos © Dwight Kuhn.

Pascoe, Elaine.
Animals with backbones / Elaine Pascoe ; photography by Dwight Kuhn.
p. cm. — (A kid's guide to the classification of living things)
Includes bibliographical references (p.   ).
Summary: Simple text and illustrations introduce the characteristics of the major groups of vertebrates: fish, amphibians, reptiles, birds, and mammals.
  ISBN 0-8239-6310-1 (lib. bdg.)
1. Vertebrates—Juvenile literature. [1. Vertebrates.] I. Kuhn, Dwight, ill.. II. Title.
  QL605.3 .P37 2003
  596—dc21
                                                                      2001005448

Manufactured in the United States of America

Contents

Sorting Living Things

Trees, insects, mushrooms, and birds are just four of the millions of different kinds of living things in the world. How do we keep track of them all? Scientists use a system called classification. Classification is a way of creating order by putting things in groups. You classify your clothes when you put them away. Socks go in one drawer and T-shirts go in another. In the same way, scientists sort living things based on the many ways in which they are alike. Most scientists sort living things into five **kingdoms**. The diagram to the right shows how a kingdom is sorted into smaller groups. The groups narrow to a single type, or **species**, of living thing. This book is about one group in the animal kingdom, animals with backbones.

The top row shows the five kingdoms. The animal kingdom can be sorted into animals with backbones and animals without backbones. Animals with backbones are sorted into fish, amphibians, reptiles, birds, and mammals. These groups can be sorted too!

Plant Kingdom

Fungus Kingdom

Animal Kingdom

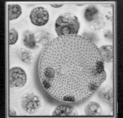

Protist Kingdom

Monera Kingdom

Animals with Backbones

Animals without Backbones

Fish

Amphibians

Reptiles

Birds

Mammals

White-Footed Mouse

Horse

Lion

Human

The Backbone Bunch

What makes a living thing an animal? Like you, all animals can move around. Animals must move to find food. Muscles and nerves help them do this. Animals use the five senses, too. They see, hear, smell, taste, and touch the world around them.

Many animals have a **spinal cord**, or a long bundle of nerves that runs down the back. The spinal cord connects the brain to the rest of the body. Animals with backbones have a row of bones that protects the spinal cord. The bones are called **vertebrae**, so animals with backbones are called **vertebrates**. Fish, frogs, snakes, sparrows, mice, and monkeys are all vertebrates. People are vertebrates, too. Can you feel your backbone?

People belong to the animal kingdom. They grow, eat, and move around to find food. They are also animals with backbones.

Fish: Swift Swimmers

Fish are vertebrates that live in oceans, rivers, streams, and lakes in every part of the world. A fish bends its backbone from side to side as it swims. This motion helps to push the fish forward through the water. Fish breathe water through **organs** called **gills**. In most fish, slits just behind the head let water into the gills.

Most fish have scaly skins. Their tails and fins help them to swim. Fish come in many shapes, sizes, and colors. The sea horse doesn't look like a fish at all, but it is!

Fish are **cold-blooded**. This means that a fish's body temperature changes with the temperature of the water around it. When the water grows colder, the fish's temperature goes down.

A goldfish and a brook trout (inset) are different in color and in shape, but they both have gills for breathing underwater and fins for swimming.

Gills

Fin

Amphibians: A Double Life

Frogs, toads, and salamanders lead double lives. These animals belong to a group of vertebrates called amphibians. Amphibians begin their lives in water, but, as adults, they live on land. Young amphibians hatch from eggs, which their mothers lay in ponds and streams. The young look like fish. They live in water and breathe through gills. Slowly they change. They grow legs so they can walk. They grow lungs so they can breathe air. Finally they leave the water for land, but these animals rarely travel far from water. Amphibians "drink" water through their thin skins. Many also take in air through their skins. This helps them breathe. Amphibians must keep their skin moist to do these things. Like fish, amphibians are cold-blooded.

Frogs' backbones are specially made for jumping. Part of a frog's backbone is made of one big bone that supports the strong hind legs.

All fish have fins and gills, and most have scales. More than half the vertebrates alive today are fish.

This goldfish has a fantail, or a double tail fin. Fantail goldfish cannot swim as fast as single-tailed goldfish.

Sea horses have one fin on their back and one on each side. They have tough skin instead of scales.

The spines on a lion fish's fancy fins hold poison. They protect the fish from predators.

Red-spotted newts are amphibians. Young red-spotted newts are called efts. Their skin color darkens as they grow older.

This wood frog tadpole has grown its legs. It will live underwater until it loses its tail. By then its gills will have closed, and its lungs will be able to breathe air.

This American toad, an animal with a backbone, is eating a worm, an animal without a backbone.

Reptiles: Sliders and Crawlers

A snake's skeleton is all backbone. Snakes have no legs. They slide on the ground. Snakes belong to the vertebrate group called reptiles. Turtles, lizards, and alligators are also reptiles. You can spot a reptile by its skin. Unlike other animals' skins, reptiles' skins are covered with either dry scales or hard plates.

Most reptiles live on land. Sea turtles and water snakes live in water, but they still must breathe air. Reptiles like to lie in the sunshine. Like fish and amphibians, they are cold-blooded. Warmth helps them move around.

Most reptiles do not take care of their young. Many lay their eggs in sheltered places and leave them. Some snakes and lizards give birth to live young, but they too leave their young right away.

Chameleons are reptiles. Within the reptile group, they belong to the lizard group. One of the chameleon's special features is its long tongue.

A hard shell made of bony plates protects the turtle. When this reptile senses danger, it pulls its head and legs inside its shell.

A green iguana can grow up to 6 ½ feet (2 m) long. Iguanas come in many sizes, but they all have dry, scaly reptile skin.

As do most reptiles, turtles lay their eggs and then leave them. When the young hatch, they are able to take care of themselves.

Snakes, such as this smooth green snake, are the only reptiles that do not have legs. However, some lizards' legs are too small to see.

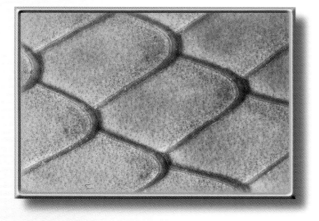

This is a close-up of a smooth green snake's scales. The outer layer of all reptiles' skin is hardened to form scales or plates.

Crocodiles and alligators are the largest living reptiles. You can tell an alligator from a crocodile by its snout. Alligators, such as this one, have wide, blunt snouts. Crocodiles' snouts are narrower.

Birds: Feathered Fliers

A peacock's feathers are fancy. A sparrow's feathers are plain. Plain or fancy, if an animal has feathers, you know it's a bird. Birds also have wings. Not all birds fly, but most do. Their backbones do not bend the way snakes' backbones do. Birds' vertebrae are joined together to keep their bodies straight when they fly.

Birds use their hard bills, or beaks, to get food. Many birds eat seeds, fruit, and other plant foods. Other birds eat insects and worms. Still others are hunters and fishers. Owls, eagles, and hawks are hunters. They catch their **prey** with their strong **talons**.

Birds live in all parts of the world. They are **warm-blooded**. This means that a bird's body temperature stays the same, no matter how warm or cold the weather. Feathers help birds stay warm in winter.

As do all birds, this saw-whet owl has feathers, wings, and a beak. Owls cannot move their eyes. They must move their entire head to look around!

Feathers

Wing

Beak

Birds: Eggs and Nests

Most birds build nests for their eggs. There are about as many different kinds of nests as there are different kinds of birds. Birds build their nests in trees, on cliffsides, on the ground, and even under ground. They guard their nests and sit on their eggs to keep them warm. Eggs come in many different sizes and colors. A robin's eggs are small and blue.

When the young birds hatch, the parents must feed them. The adults are busy all day, bringing food to the hungry hatchlings. Sometimes only the mother bird builds the nest and cares for the young, but often the mother and the father share the job. The work goes on until the young are old enough to leave the nest and to find their own food.

The eggs in this robin's nest (inset) will soon hatch into baby robins. This adult robin built a nest of twigs and grass for her young.

Puffins are ocean birds that dive underwater to catch fish. A puffin can hold 12 or more small fish in its bill at one time!

A Savannah sparrow sings from its perch. There are as many different birdsongs as there are types of birds.

The colorful feathers on a peacock, a male peafowl, help it to attract females.

Hummingbirds make their nests from bits of plants and spiderwebs. This mother hummingbird is feeding her young.

Mute swans are born with soft, gray feathers called down. Their first true feathers are brown. White feathers grow in by the time the swans are a year old.

Mammals: Milk and More

How is a little hedgehog like a fierce tiger? Both belong to the vertebrate group called mammals. Cats, bats, deer, mice, and many other creatures belong to this group. Whales and dolphins are mammals that spend their lives in water. They come to the surface to breathe air. You are a mammal, too.

How can you tell if an animal is a mammal? Mammals are the only animals that **nurse** their young. They are also the only animals with hair. Some have very little hair, but many are covered in thick hair we call fur. Like birds, mammals are warm-blooded. Hair helps them to stay warm.

Mammals have keen senses and large brains. The smartest animals of all, dolphins, apes, and people, are mammals.

Horses are mammals. They have fur, breathe air, and feed milk to their young. This baby horse, or foal, is drinking milk from its mother.

Mammals: Caring for Young

Baby mammals need a lot of care. Newborn mice are hairless and blind. Their mother cares for them in a nest. If she must move them, she carries them gently in her mouth. Within two weeks, the babies' eyes open. They grow fur and scamper around.

A mother mouse, a mother horse, and all other mammal moms give milk to their babies. The milk is produced by **mammary glands** in the mother's body. Even when the youngsters begin to eat other foods, mammal parents often keep caring for their young. The parents teach them the skills they need to find food and to **survive** on their own.

Unlike reptile babies, mammal babies are not able to take care of themselves as soon as they are born. If baby mice are in danger, their mother will carry them to a safe place, one by one.

All mammals have hair, but their hair comes in many colors and thicknesses and can feel very different. A lion's hair feels something like a dog's hair.

The hair of a hedgehog feels stiff and prickly. It helps to protect the hedgehog from animals that might want to eat it.

A ring-tailed lemur's fur is thick and soft. It feels a bit like a cat's fur.

Life's Common Threads

Animals with backbones are just one group of the many living things on Earth. All living things are alike in some important ways. Just as you grow taller each year, all living things grow and change. They also **reproduce**. A chicken lays eggs that hatch into chicks. A maple tree forms seeds that sprout into new maple trees.

Living things need food. Plants make their own food. Other living things must get food from somewhere. Living things sense the world around them. All living things, even plants, react to what they sense.

Nonliving things can do none of these things. Your chair can't grow or make more chairs. It doesn't eat, and it doesn't know when you sit on it. Only living things have these abilities.

Rocks are nonliving things. They don't move on their own. They don't need food, and they don't reproduce.

Glossary

cold-blooded (KOLD-bluh-did) Having a body temperature that changes with the surrounding temperature.

gills (GILZ) Body parts for taking oxygen from water, or breathing water.

kingdoms (KEENG-duhmz) The first level of groups into which scientists sort living things.

mammary glands (MA-muh-ree GLANDZ) Body parts that produce milk.

nurse (NURS) When a female feeds her baby milk from her body.

organs (OR-gunz) Parts inside the body, such as the heart and lungs.

prey (PRAY) Animals that are hunted by other animals for food.

reproduce (ree-pruh-DOOS) To have babies.

species (SPEE-sheez) The smallest grouping in the classification of living things.

spinal cord (SPY-nuhl KORD) A long bundle of nerves that runs down the back and carries messages between the brain and the rest of the body.

survive (sur-VYV) To stay alive.

talons (TA-lunz) The strong, sharp-clawed feet of a bird that eats animals.

vertebrae (VER-tuh-bray) Backbones, which protect the spinal cord.

vertebrates (VER-tih-brits) Animals that have backbones.

warm-blooded (WORM-bluh-did) Having a body temperature that stays the same, no matter what the surrounding temperature.

Index

Web Sites

To learn more about classification and animals with backbones, check out these Web sites:

www.hhmi.org/coolscience
www.kapili.com/t/taxonomy.html
www.perspective.com/nature/index.html